P9-CQK-399

Two years ago, Rosie O'Donnell asked kids to send her their best jokes—and woke up to a mailbox overflowing with thousands of riddles, puns, and drawings from her youngest fans. Rosie told their jokes on her show and collected her favorites for *Kids Are Punny,* which became an immediate bestseller. But the flood of mail—and kidding around—continued! Now to share some more of the fun, Rosie presents KIDS ARE PUNNY 2, more than a hundred great new jokes sure to make you grin, groan, and giggle . . . all from the shortest and punniest people on the planet—kids!

All profits from this book go to the For All Kids Foundation, P.O. Box 225, Allendale, NJ 07401, which is devoted to children's charities.

Zlatan Zukanovic, age 14

Kids are Funny 2

More Jokes Sent by Kids to
The Rosie O'Donnell Show

WARNER BOOKS

A Time Warner Company

Warner Books, Inc., 1271 Avenue of the Americas, New York, NY 10020
Visit our Web site at http://warnerbooks.com

A Time Warner Company

Printed in the United States of America

First Printing: October 1998

10   9   8   7   6   5   4   3   2   1

ISBN: 0-446-52540-5
LC: 98-87008

Text design by Stanley S. Drate/Folio Graphics Co. Inc.
Front and back cover photos by Herman Estevez

Contents

Introduction
by Rosie O'Donnell

Hello all,

Book 2—who woulda thunk it?

Here are the latest jokes, sent in by you, the coolest kids on the planet.

Read 'em, know 'em, tell 'em.

Hey, writers, rock on. You kids are punny, and in the process raised over 1 million dollars to help kids in need. Here's hoping this book can raise even more.

I once heard a story about a young boy. He spent his days on the beach, throwing starfish back into the water. An old man approached him and asked what he was doing.

"I am throwing these starfish back in the water before the sun dries them out and they die."

The old man shook his head. "Look down the beach, son. There are too many starfish. You cannot save them all, so it does not matter." As the old man walked away, the boy picked up a starfish and threw it back into the water.

"It does to this one," he said.

Thank you all for throwing starfish.

Wild and Woolly

Why did the lion eat the tightrope walker?

He wanted a well-balanced meal.

Bridget Marie Guzman, age 9

Why is it so hard to hide a leopard?
Because they're always spotted.

Jordan Rivera, age 7

What is yellow and black with red spots?

A leopard with the measles.

◆

What do you get when you cross a snowman with a tiger?

Frostbite.

Karen Zhang, age 5

Why were the elephants thrown out of the swimming pool?

Because they couldn't keep their trunks up.

♦

Why are elephants so wrinkled?

Have you ever tried to iron one?

♦

How do you know when there is an elephant under your bed?

When your nose touches the ceiling.

♦

What's the difference between an elephant and a flea?

An elephant can have fleas but a flea can't have elephants.

♦

What do you call an elephant who flies?

A jumbo jet.

What do you get when you cross an elephant and a computer?

A five-ton know-it-all.

◆

What do you call a sick alligator?

An illigator.

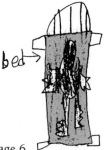

Scott Malinowski, age 6

What do you do when you're stuck inside an elephant?

Run around 'til you're all pooped out.

Lindsay, Jordan, and Kelsey Kurlin, ages 16, 8, 6

What did the kangaroo say when she couldn't find her baby?

Someone has picked my pocket.

How do camels hide in the desert?

With camel-flage!

Dominika Skirlo, age 6

What was the name of the camel without a hump?

Humphrey.

◆

Why don't anteaters ever get sick?

Because they are full of antibodies.

◆

What did the mother buffalo say to her baby when he went off to school?

Bison.

Really Stinky Jokes

What do you call a room with 50 pigs on one side and 50 deer on the other?

100 sows and bucks.

◆

What do pigs put into their computers?

Sloppy disks.

Leah Rosenblatt, age 12

How do you stop a skunk from smelling?

Hold his nose.

✦

What happened when the skunk wrote a book?

It became a best smeller.

What does the Pig say when he has a heart attack?

Joshua Young, age 6

On the Farm

Why do sheep make bad drivers?

They make too many ewe turns.

What is a sheep's favorite fruit?

Baaa-nana.

Why don't ducks tell jokes in the air?

Because they would quack up.

Erin Maxwell, age 11

What do you call a crate of ducks?

A box of quackers.

What is the best bird for boxing?

Duck!

Why did the chicken join the band?

Because he had his own pair of drumsticks.

What kind of suit does a duck wear?

A duck-seedo.

Daniel Maxwell, age 9

How do you stuff a turkey?

Feed him a lot of food.

Rosanne Romanello, age 11

Why did the chicken cross the road, roll in the dirt, and cross the road again?

Because he is a dirty double-crosser.

◆

What do you call a chicken who thinks he's Superman?

Cluck Kent.

◆

What kind of horse collects stamps?

A hobby horse.

◆

What does a horse say when she's finished eating her hay?

That's the last straw.

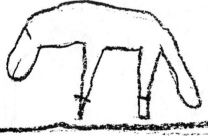

Karen Zhang, age 5

What does a horse put on her head on a bad hair day?

Hay spray.

◆

What's white, loves cheese, and has a trunk?

A mouse going on vacation.

◆

Where do little cows eat?

In the calf-eteria.

Bridget Marie Guzman, age 9

What do mice do during the day?

Mousework.

◆

What do you get when you cross a hummingbird with a cow?

A humburger.

◆

What do you give a deer for an upset stomach?

Elk-a-seltzer.

◆

What do you call a rabbit who is owned by a beetle?

A bug's bunny.

◆

What makes a rabbit grumpy?

A bad hare day.

Creepy Crawlies

Snake #1: I hope I am not poisonous.
Snake #2: Why?
Snake #1: Because I just bit my tongue.

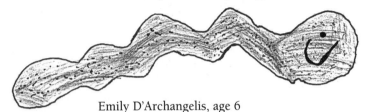

Emily D'Archangelis, age 6

What is a snake's favorite subject?

Hiss-story.

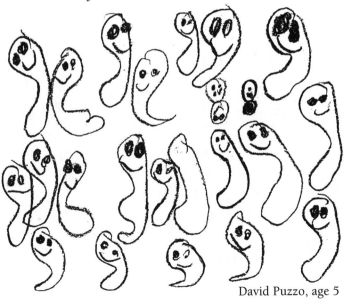

David Puzzo, age 5

What do you get when you cross a snake with a magician?

Abra da cobra.

◆

Why did the baby snake cry?

Because he lost his rattle.

◆

What was the tortoise doing on the highway?

About 150 inches an hour.

◆

What did the turtle wear to keep warm?

A people-neck sweater.

Michael, Nick, and Theresa Toth, ages 9, 7, and 4

What do you get when you cross a turtle with a porcupine?

A slow poke.

◆

What is a frog's favorite winter game?

Ice hoppy.

Sarah D'Archangelis, age 10

What do frogs wear on their feet in the summer?

Open-toad shoes.

◆

Why are frogs so happy?

They eat whatever bugs them.

15

What's white outside, green inside, and hops?

A frog sandwich.

◆

What does a frog do to paper?

Rippit!

◆

Where do you take a frog with bad eyesight?

To the hoptician.

Susan Kraus, age 7

What happens to frogs left in a no-parking zone?

They get toad away.

◆

Why couldn't the worms go on the ark in an apple?

Because they had to go in pears.

Something's Fishy

Why did the dolphin feel so sad?

Because his life had no porpoise.

Christopher Chin, age 8

What is a shark's favorite game?

Swallow the leader.

◆

What did the sardine call the submarine?

A can of people.

Nico Martiny, age 8

What happened to the sardine when she didn't show up for work?

She was canned.

What do you get from a bad-tempered shark?

As far away as possible.

◆

What is a shark's favorite sandwich?

A submarine.

◆

Where do sharks come from?

Shark-ago.

◆

What did Cinderella Seal wear to the ball?

Glass flippers.

◆

Why do fish live in salt water?

Because pepper makes them sneeze.

James Rinaldi, age 10

For the Birds

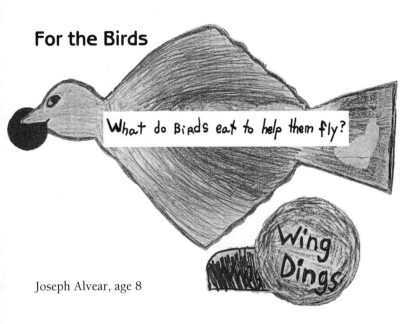

What do Birds eat to help them fly?

Wing Dings

Joseph Alvear, age 8

What bird is with you at every meal?

A swallow.

How do robins get in shape?

They do worm-ups.

How do baby hens dance?

Chick to chick.

What happens when two geese have a head-on collision?

They get goose bumps.

Kara Ali Goldsmith, age 8

What kind of birds jump out of airplanes?

Parrot troopers.

◆

What do you get when you cross a parrot and a pig?

A bird who hogs the conversation.

These'll Bug You

What do termites do when they need a rest?

They take a coffee-table break.

◆

What is the biggest ant?

An elephant.

Samantha Wolff, age 8

Why was the baby ant so confused?

Because all of his uncles were ants.

◆

What bee can never be understood?

A mumblebee.

What does a bee wear when he goes jogging?

A swarm-up suit.

What do you get when you cross a seagull and a bee?

A beagle.

What do insects learn in school?

Moth-e-matics.

Emily D'Archangelis, age 6

Who built the first underground tunnel?

A worm.

Why do spiders spin webs?

Because they don't know how to knit.

Bow-WOWS

What do you call a dog who likes science experiments?

A lab-rador!

Julia Freeman, age 4

What do you call a sick dog?

A germy shepherd.

what do you call a puppy with a bad temper?

Joseph Alvear, age 8

A devil dog.

What is a theme park for dogs?

Jurassic Bark.

Niall O'Riordan, age 6

What goes *tick-tock, bow-wow, tick-tock, bow-wow*?

A watchdog.

◆

What does a dog do that a man steps in?

Pants.

What kind of market does a dog hate?

A flea market.

Kathryn Sutcliffe, age 5

What's cute, furry, barks, and is frozen on a stick?

A pup-cicle!

Meow-WOWS

What did the cat receive after it made a movie?

Tanya Alvear, age 10

An A-cat-emy Award!

What part of the tree scared the cat?

Its bark.

◆

What do cats serve at birthday parties?

Cake and mice cream.

What happened to the cat who swallowed a ball of yarn?

She had mittens.

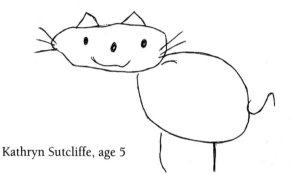

Kathryn Sutcliffe, age 5

How do you make a cat float?

Two scoops of ice cream, some root beer, and a cat!

What do you call a cat who pouts?

A sour puss.

Where do cats like to hide?

In the clawset.

What did the cat say
when she burned her tail?

This is the end of me!

Kara Ali Goldsmith, age 8

OLD FAVORITES

What kind of van does Minnie Mouse drive?

A minivan.

Donyetta Cottle

What do you get when you throw Daffy Duck in the Atlantic Ocean?

Saltwater Daffy.

◆

Why did Donald Duck go to medical school?

He wanted to be a wise quacker.

Where does Batman take a shower?

In the batroom.

Dylan O'Keefe, age 6½

Why can't Batman and Robin go fishing together?

Robin will eat all the worms.

◆

What spaceman will always lend you a dollar?

Buck Rogers.

What do you get when you cross a bear with a skunk?

Winnie the Pooh.

❖

What do Winnie the Pooh and Kermit the Frog have in common?

They both have the same middle name.

❖

What is Tarzan's favorite Christmas carol?

"Jungle Bells."

❖

Why did Humpty Dumpty have a great fall?

To make up for a lousy summer.

❖

What do you call a pretty girl using a broom?

Sweeping Beauty.

Why didn't Cinderella join the baseball team?

Because she ran away from the ball.

Melissa Ross, age 8

Why did King Kong climb the Empire State Building?

Because he had to catch a plane.

Garrett Nondorf, age 6

Andrew Davino, age 13

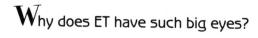

Why does ET have such big eyes?

You would, too, if you saw his phone bill.

Anthony Davino, age 8

What is furry, red, and comes in a jar?

Pickle me Elmo.

✦

Why was Ariel upset after playing hide-and-seek?

Because Sebastian Flounder.

✦

What is a detective in a bubble bath called?

Sherlock Foams.

✦

What do you get when you cross *Jeopardy!* with a dinosaur?

Alex T-Rex.

✦

Which dinosaur is the noisiest sleeper?

Bronto-snorus.

✦

What is brown and lives in the bell tower?

The lunchbag of Notre Dame.

What pirate wore expensive underwear?

Long John Silver.

Susan Kraus, age 7

What rock star likes to shop the most?

Buyin' Adams.

Bobby Penn, age 6

HISTORY QUIZ

What is round and purple and almost conquered the world?

Alexander the Grape.

Tamar Golan, age 9

What did George Washington's father say when he saw his report card?

You're going down in history.

What dance did the Pilgrims do?

Plymouth Rock.

Niall O'Riordan, age 6

Where did Lincoln write the Gettysburg Address?

On an envelope.

FOOLISH, GHOULISH JOKES

Ryan Irwin, age 9

Why do ghosts like to ride elevators?

It raises their spirits.

◆

What is a ghost's favorite sandwich?

Boo-logna!

◆

How do ghosts like their eggs?

Terri-fried.

What does a ghost use to go hunting?

A boo and arrow.

Gaspare Chiarenza, age 6

What baseball team do ghosts like best?

The Toronto Boo Jays.

◆

What kind of pants do ghosts wear?

Boo jeans.

◆

What happens when a ghost haunts Broadway?

The actors get stage fright!

What is Dracula's favorite sport?

Casketball.

◆

What did Dracula say about his girlfriend?

It was love at first bite.

Clare McKeon, age 9

Where does Dracula go to work?

The Vampire State Building.

◆

What did one skeleton say to the other skeleton?

I've got a bone to pick with you.

What do skeletons say before dining?

Bone appétit!

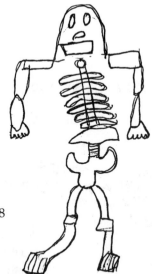

Christopher Chin, age 8

Which school subject was the witch good at?

Spell-ing.

◆

What kind of witch lives at the beach?

A sand-witch.

◆

What is the best way to speak to a monster?

From far, far away.

What did one casket say to the other?

Is that you coffin?!

◆

Why do mummies go to school?

To get a dead-ucation.

◆

What do you call a staircase in a haunted house?

A scare-case.

Courtney Harris, age 10

What's the scariest waterway in America?

The Erie Canal.

What does a piece of toast wear to bed?

Its jam-mies.

◆

Where were the first french fries made?

In Greece.

What do you call two banana peels?

A pair of slippers!

Emily D'Archangelis, age 6

What is a computer's favorite food?

Chips.

◆

Where did the hamburgers go to dance?

The meatball.

◆

Why was the sweet potato not allowed to marry the TV reporter?

Because he was just a common tater.

Analiese Michelle Flores, age 7

Why did the hot dog win the race?

Because he was the wiener.

Lola Dalrymple, age 9

What vegetable would you least want on a boat?

A leek!

◆

What do you call a carrot who talks back?

A fresh vegetable.

◆

Why didn't the cucumber want to become a pickle?

It was too jarring.

◆

What kind of fruit do you find on ships?

Naval oranges.

Where do cantaloupes go for the summer?

John Cougar Meloncamp.

✦

What did one strawberry say to the other strawberry?

If you weren't so fresh, we wouldn't be in this jam.

✦

What do you call a rich melon?

A melon-aire.

✦

Why did the jelly roll?

To see the apple turnover.

✦

Why did the banana go out with the prune?

Because he couldn't get a date.

What did the egg say
when he burped?

Egg-scuse me!

Aedan McCarty, age 4

What do you get when you cross a lighthouse
and a hen house?

Beacon and eggs.

✦

How did the egg cross the road?

She scrambled across.

✦

What did one pig say to the other in the
summer?

I'm bacon.

Why was it cold in the school cafeteria?

Because they were serving burritos and chili.

◆

What do you call a person who can't flip pancakes?

A flip flop.

Jane Harvey, age 8

What do people in the Midwest drink?

Minne-soda.

◆

What are two things you can never eat for breakfast?

Lunch and supper.

THE SICKEST JOKES
WE KNOW

What is the difference between a dentist and a New York Yankees fan?

One roots for the Yanks and one yanks for the roots.

◆

When a boat is sick, where does it go?

To the dock.

◆

What did the monster eat after the dentist pulled out his tooth?

The dentist.

Susan Kraus, age 7

What did one tonsil say to the other tonsil?

Get dressed, the doctor is taking us out tonight.

◆

What do you call a dentist who offers to clean a werewolf's teeth?

Crazy!

◆

At what time do most people visit the dentist?

Tooth-hurty.

Johnny Mendez, age 5

What did the dentist give to the marching band?

A tuba toothpaste.

Kathryn Ware, age 8

Why did the leaf go to the doctor?

He was a little green.

✦

Why are doctors so calm?

Because they have a lot of patients.

HOME HUMOR

What did the broom say to the vacuum cleaner?

I wish people would stop pushing us around.

Jugan Selvatatsam, age 8

What gets wetter the more it dries?

A towel.

JOKES THAT'LL DRIVE YOU CRAZY

What does a car wear when it's cold?

A cardigan.

◆

What kind of song do you sing in a car?

A cartune.

Nico Martiny, age 8

What do you get when you cross a rainstorm and a convertible?

A carpool.

◆

What kind of car does a farmer drive?

A cornvertible.

What do you get when you cross a motorcycle with a joke book?

A Yamahahahaha!

✦

What kind of car does an electrician drive?

A voltswagon.

Stephen Knips, age 8

Why did the car have a stomachache?

It had too much gas.

✦

Why are barbers the best race car drivers?

Because they know all the short cuts.

JUST PLAYING AROUND

What do you call a fat football player and a pay phone put together?

A wide receiver.

Michael McGee, age 10

What did the baseball glove say to the baseball?

Catch you later.

◆

What kind of ball can you serve but not eat?

A volleyball.

◆

What do you call a frightened scuba diver?

Chicken of the sea.

◆

What do you call a yo-yo that doesn't come back up?

A yo!

◆

Why can't you play cards on a small boat?

Someone's always sitting on the deck.

Daniel Maxwell, age 8

Why shouldn't you tell a joke while you are ice skating?

The ice might crack up.

Why was Michael Jordan always sleeping?

He was part of the Dream Team

Frank Romanello, age 8

OUT OF THIS WORLD

How does the man in the moon cut his hair?

Eclipse it.

Dylan O'Keefe, age 6½

Why wasn't the moon full last night?

Because it didn't eat all its dinner.

◆

What extraterrestrial likes to visit the ocean?

An eel-ian.

How do you get a baby astronaut to go to sleep?

You rock-et.

✦

What did the astronaut see in his frying pan?

An unidentified frying object.

Brian Crawford, age 6

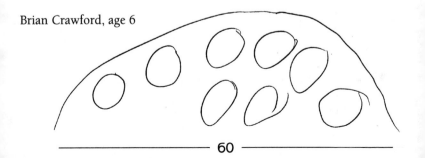

What game do astronauts like to play?

Moon-opoly.

✦

What do astronauts eat for lunch?

Launch meat sandwiches.

✦

What does an astronaut do when he gets dirty?

He takes a meteor shower.

✦

What kind of music do Martians listen to?

Neptunes.

Sarah D'Archangelis, age 10

NATURE CALLS

Why couldn't the flower ride his bike?

He lost his petals.

◆

What did the big flower say to the little flower?

Hi, bud.

Lauren Ferrando, age 9

Where is the best place to grow flowers in school?

In the kinder-garden.

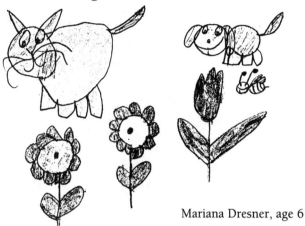

Mariana Dresner, age 6

What did the porcupine say to the cactus?

Is that you, Mama?

✦

What has bark but no bite?

A tree.

✦

Why didn't the tree answer the question?

Because he was stumped.

What do you call a half-grown tree?

A tree-nager.

Cody Philhower, age 7

What tree can give you a high five?

A palm tree.

◆

What do you get when you cross a karate expert with a tree?

Spruce Lee.

◆

What is the best way to paint the ocean?

With watercolors.

What bow can never be tied?

A rainbow.

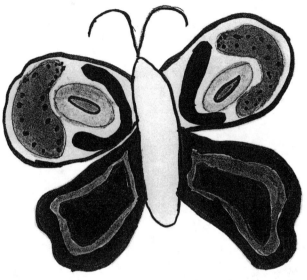

Katherine Nondorf, age 8

What did one earthquake say to the other earthquake?

It's not my fault.

◆

Why does lightning shock people?

Because it doesn't know how to conduct itself.

What does a rain cloud wear under its coat?

Thunderwear.

Maggie White, age 6

What did the river say to the sea?

It was nice running into you!

DUMB QUESTIONS/
SMART ANSWERS

What disasters happen every 24 hours?

Day breaks and night falls.

Why did the little girl sit on her watch?

She wanted to be on time.

Daniela Lucero, age 5

Where does the general keep his armies?

Up his sleevies.

When is a door not a door?

When it is ajar.

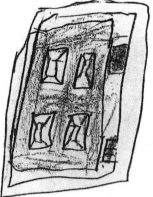

Thomas McDonald, age 7

What is a Slinky's favorite season?

Spring!

◆

Why did the lady sit in her rocking chair with her roller skates on?

She wanted to rock and roll.

◆

What did one toilet say to the other one?

You look flushed.

Why are Saturday and Sunday the strongest days?

Because all the rest are weak days.

✦

Is this milk pasteurized?

No, it's only up to my nose!

✦

What do you get when you cross an artist with a slob?

A messterpiece.

✦

How does a wig introduce itself?

Hair I am.

✦

What always sleeps through dinner?

A nap-kin.

What is the hardest thing about skydiving?

The ground.

Brian Crawford, age 6

What is the richest air?

A million-aire.

◆

What do you call a dinosaur that explodes?

Dino-mite!

◆

What has a head, a tail, and no body?

A penny.

What animal are you like when you take a bath?

A little bear.

Jackie Hanauer, age 7

Where did the plumber go on vacation?

Flushing, New York.

◆

Who's bigger, Mr. Bigger or Mr. Bigger's baby?

Mr. Bigger's baby is just a little Bigger.

What is the same about false teeth and stars?

They both come out at night.

Kayla McKoy, age 8

◆

What is of most use when it is used up?

An umbrella.

◆

What letter is always the center of attention?

The letter "n."

where do computers go to dance?

a disk-o

Jaime Campbell, age 11

KNOCK-KNOCK

Knock-knock.
Who's there?
Arthur.
Arthur who?
Arthur any more Ring Dings in the house?

◆

Knock-knock.
Who's there?
Jamaica.
Jamaica who?
Jamaica my lunch yet?

◆

Knock-knock.
Who's there?
Cargo.
Cargo who?
Cargo beep beep.

Malorie Lakosky, age 6

Knock-knock.
Who's there?
Juicy.
Juicy who?
Juicy the hockey game last night?

Knock-knock.
Who's there?
Little old lady.
Little old lady who?
I didn't know you could yodel!

Knock-knock.
Who's there?
RV.
RV who?
RV there yet??!

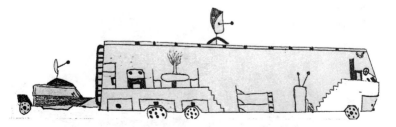

Rasaan Bonair, age 11

Knock-knock.
Who's there?
Someone too short to ring the bell.

◆

Knock-knock.
Who's there?
Justin.
Justin who?
Justin time for dinner.

◆

Knock-knock.
Who's there?
House.
House who?
House you doing?

Robert White, age 8

Knock-knock.
Who's there?
Disguise.
Disguise who?
Disguise the limit.

◆

Knock-knock.
Who's there?
Zombies.
Zombies who?
Zombies make honey
    and zombies don't.

Aedan McCarty, age 4

Knock-knock.
Who's there?
Amarillo.
Amarillo who?
Amarillo fashioned cowboy.

Knock-knock.
Who's there?
Yule.
Yule who?
Yule never know unless you open the door.

Knock-knock.
Who's there?
Ammonia.
Ammonia who?
Ammonia kidding. I don't want to come in.

Knock-knock.
Who's there?
Atlas.
Atlas who?
Atlas I'm here.

Knock-knock.
Who's there?
Ooze.
Ooze who?
Ooze in charge around here?

Samantha Wolff, age 8

Knock-knock.
Who's there?
Jess.
Jess who?
Jess me.

Knock-knock.
Who's there?
Lena.
Lena who?
Lena little closer and I won't have to yell.

Knock-knock.
Who's there?
Believing.
Believing who?
Open the door or I'll believing.

Knock-knock.
Who's there?
Avenue.
Avenue who?
Avenue heard this joke before?

Knock-knock.
Who's there?
Cereal.
Cereal who?
Cereal soon.

Knock-knock.
Who's there?
Sarah.
Sarah who?
Sarah doctor in the house?

Knock-knock.
Who's there?
Althea.
Althea who?
Althea later, alligator.

Merrill McIntire, age 7

Knock-knock.
Who's there?
Wanda.
Wanda who?
I wanda be your friend!

Natalia Calderon, age 6

Knock-knock.
Who's there?
Heaven.
Heaven who?
Heaven you heard enough of these knock-knock
   jokes?

ROSIE

What would Rosie be if she were being chased by a man-eating tiger?

Glad she's a woman.

Kate Miller, age 11

Knock-knock.
Who's there?
Norma Lee.
Norma Lee who?
Norma Lee I don't go around knocking on people's
   doors but I just had to say: Hello, Rosie!

Lauren Ferrando, age 9

What is the difference between Rosie and her car?

Her car has Cruise control.

◆

Knock-knock.
Who's there?
Ura.
Ura who?
Ura funny person, Rosie!

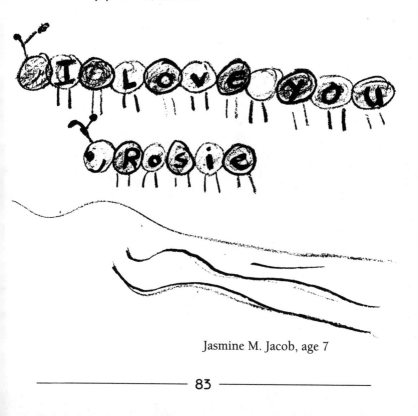

Jasmine M. Jacob, age 7

My Special Thanks
to All of the Children Who Sent in Their Great Jokes and Pictures!

Aaron	Charlie	Gwynne	Katie
Adam	Chloe	Harley	Kayla
Aidan	Chris	Heather	Kellie
Alexander	Christina	Jack	Kelsy
Alexis	Christine	Jake	Kenny
Ali	Clair	Jamie	Kerry
Allison	Cody	Jason	Kevin
Alyssa	Colin	Jen	Kristen
Amy	Dana	Jennifer	Krysta
Analiese	Danielle	Jenny	Kyle
Andrew	Danny	Jessica	Langley
Anthony	Dave	Jillian	Laura
April	Deana	John	Lauren
Ariel	Douglas	Johnny	Lexi
Ashley	Dree	Jordan	Lindsay
Asia	Elise	Joseph	Luke
Brandon	Elissa	Joshua	Maireade
Brian	Elizabeth	Josie	Mallori
Brianna	Elyse	Jugan	Malorie
Bridgette	Emily	Julia	Marc
Bridie	Emma	Julianne	Matthew
Brittany	Garrett	Justin	Maura
Caitlin	Gianni	Kari	Megan
Carla	Gina	Kate	Michael
Carly	Gino	Katelyn	Michelle
Cayleigh	Grace	Katherine	Nicholas
Charles	Graydon	Kathryn	Nicole

Niko
Noelle
Patrick
Peter
Priscilla
Robbie
Robert
Romeo
Ryan
Sam

Samantha
Sammy
Sarah
Sarah-Jane
Scott
Shaun
Shayne
Stefanie
Stephanie
Steven

Sydney
Tanner
Tanya
Tara
Taylor
Theresa
Tiana
Tiffany
Timmy
Tracey

Trez
Tristan
Tyler
Vandana
Vincent
William
Woo Rim
Zlatan